SATURN

PLANETS IN OUR SOLAR SYSTEM

CHILDREN'S ASTRONOMY EDITION

SPEEDY PUBLISHING

Speedy Publishing LLC
40 E. Main St. #1156
Newark, DE 19711
www.speedypublishing.com

Saturn is the sixth
planet from the Sun.

Saturn is the second-largest planet in the Solar System with an average radius about nine times that of Earth.

Saturn is the lightest planet.

Saturn is named after the Roman god of agriculture. He was called Cronus by the Greeks.

If there was a bathtub big enough to hold Saturn, it would float in the water!

Saturn has a small rocky core covered with liquid gas that is composed of hydrogen and helium.

Saturn has a hot interior, reaching 11,700 °C at its core.

Saturn has a ring system that consists of nine continuous main rings and three discontinuous arcs and that is composed mostly of ice particles.

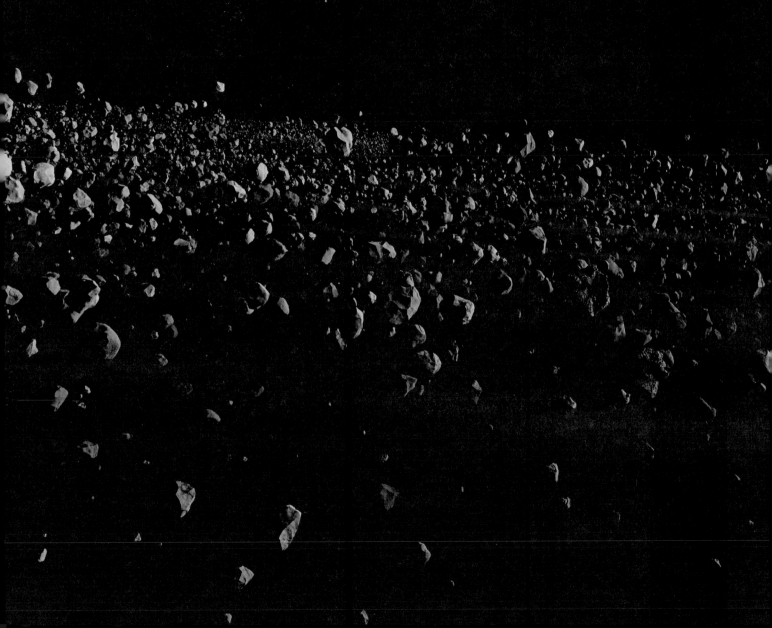

Saturn is the
flattest planet.

Saturn is not a peaceful planet. Storm winds race around the atmosphere at 800 kilometers per hour.

Saturn's upper atmosphere is divided into bands of clouds.

The average distance between Saturn and the Sun is over 1.4 billion kilometres.

Many of Saturn's moons are named after the Titans.

Saturn takes
29 and a
half years
to make one
complete orbit
of the Sun.

Saturn is the furthest planet from Earth that can be seen without the help of a telescope.

Saturn has 53 official moons and 9 provisional moons. This does not include the hundreds of moonlets comprising the rings.

Saturn's axis is tilted and as the planet orbits the Sun we get different views of the rings.

Saturn completes a full rotation on its axis in just over 10 hours.

Galileo originally called Saturn's rings "ears."